Jenny Bristow's
Country Cooking

JENNY BRISTOW'S

COUNTRY COOKING

APPLETREE PRESS

For Rosie

First published by
The Appletree Press Ltd
19-21 Alfred Street
Belfast BT2 8DL
1996.

Text © Jenny Bristow, 1996
Photographs © The Appletree Press Ltd, 1996

Photography: Robert McKeag Studios
Food stylist: Anne Bryan
Illustrations: Des Fox
Printed in Ireland

A catalogue record for this book
is available from the British Library.

ISBN 0 86281 645 9

Contents

Acknowledgements

This book and television series would certainly not exist without the help, advice and "threats" of many people.

Credit for the original idea for the series goes to Ruth Johnston, who as a long-time friend, and no mean cook herself, both produced and directed the television series. Ruth thankfully has learned to remain remarkably calm throughout the filming, coping not only with me and the crew, but with my husband, Bobby, and three children. She also somehow managed to convince them that they should all be somewhere else well before 9a.m.

Thanks also go to Mike McCann, Head of Public Affairs at UTV, for his hard work and humour in the co-ordination of the book with the series. Your help has been much appreciated.

On the home front, my heartfelt thanks to Maureen Best and Sally Stirling for their invaluable help preparing the food for the recipes, keeping the kitchen, cupboards and myself in order, and finding pots and pans I knew were there somewhere. All part of the fun of making a television series at home. Thanks also to Maureen's sister, Vera McCready, who typed the text for this book.

To the UTV film crew: Sam Christie, Rai Woods, Ken McNally, Maurice Blair, Brian Armstrong, Patricia Moore, Joan Calvert and Mary McCleave.

The food photography team at Robert McKeag Studios - Robert McKeag and Howard Ward, and food stylist Anne Bryan.

Special thanks to The Appletree Press publishing team: John Murphy, publisher and Nicola Lavery, editor.

For the variety of dishes, pans, jugs & utensils my thanks to: David Flynn of Marlborough Antiques (Belfast); Nicholas Mosse Pottery (Kilkenny); Christine Foy from Mullaghmeen Pottery (Enniskillen); Michelle Kershaw of Lakeland Plastics; June Chesney at Chesney Antiques (Portglenone); Tory, Barbara and Sheila at Habitat (Belfast); Anne and Robin at Debenhams (Belfast); Catherine McMillan at Beech Grove Interiors (Ballymena); Ian Thompson Mew Gallery (Comber); Anthea at Herbert Gould (Holywood); Ken Crockett at Balmoral Flowers; Rhoda Quinn at She Shop (Belfast); Ian McKay at Calor Gas; Bronagh Rooney at Fyffes; D. J. Lockhart, Platinum Homewares Lagostina; Cuisine Cookware; Le Creuset; and Joanne Hughes.

Thanks also to Sally Backus for the fresh flower arrangements and Lorna Bassett for the dried flowers and garlands.

I would also like to thank everyone at UTV for their encouragement and support during the making of our fifth television series and the writing of this book.

Introduction

The flavours of Country Cooking are drawn from all around the world, but that doesn't mean you have to do a spot of globe-trotting to get the ingredients. As you have probably noticed, our supermarkets are now full of new and exciting foods, and the variety of products available has increased dramatically over the past few years. I used to be able to whip around a supermarket and do my shopping in no time at all, but nowadays it takes me longer. I don't believe that it has anything to do with me slowing down slightly, but rather it is due to the huge selection of new and trendy foods that are displayed on the shelves.

Every year that passes I find my cupboards and shelves becoming stacked with new products. Five years ago I didn't have fresh herbs on my kitchen window sill, limes tucked happily alongside peppers of every colour, a selection of cooking oils or vinegars able to bring out the flavour of strawberries as well as chipped potatoes! Never before has there been such a choice of new foods stacked alongside ketchups, cordials, cucumbers and countless other familiar favourites.

But, before you panic, this is not a book of foreign or fancy cookery, nor do I have any claim to being an expert on French, Italian or Chinese cuisine. It is instead an enthusiastic journey with our new ingredients, explaining how to choose and get the best from them, prepare them and create many wonderful dishes that don't take a lifetime to make. There are many new ideas: couscous-coated crab cakes; quick and spicy curries from India and creamier ones from the Caribbean; kebabs from Portugal - piri piri-style; a chicken dish from Italy that uses Mascarpone cheese; chowder and gumbo from America; berry pudding from Greece; and exotic fruit from the Caribbean dipped in a coconut and caramel sauce.

We're making more use of spices and herbs in today's cooking and you'll probably be surprised just how many of them you have tucked away in a dark cupboard somewhere! But a word of warning, commercial spices and dried herbs tend to lose their flavour after six months so remember to replace them. Even better, try using fresh herbs or spices - you will soon discover what works best with fish, chicken or pork and will add a whole new dimension to your cooking.

As I said before, this book is not designed to send you off on an unending shopping spree, but rather encourage you to try some of the exciting, new ingredients to be found in most supermarkets.

Jenny Bristow

Conversion of Measurements

The following equivalents were used in converting between metric and imperial measurements.

Temperature

Temp°C	Temp°F	Gas Mark
110	225	¼
120	250	½
140	275	1
150	300	2
160	325	3
180	350	4
190	375	5
200	400	6
220	425	7
230	450	8
240	475	9

Volume

Vol ml/L	Vol Pt/ fl oz
3.40L	6pt
2.75L	5pt
2.25L	4pt
1.7L	3pt
1.4L	2½pt
1.1L	2pt
850ml	1½pt
570ml	1pt
425ml	¾pt
380ml	⅔pt
280ml	½pt
200ml	7fl oz
170ml	6fl oz
140ml	¼pt
115ml	4fl oz
70ml	⅛pt

Weight

Weight Kg	Weight lb
1.35kg	3lb
900g	2lb
680g	1½lb
450g	1lb
400g	14oz
340g	12oz
285g	10oz
225g	8oz
200g	7oz
170g	6oz
140g	5oz
115g	4oz
85g	3oz
70g	2½ oz
55g	2oz
45g	1½oz
30g	1oz
15g	½oz

American Pie

You know, a few years ago I didn't have salsas, chillies, peppers, yoghurt, pestos, oils or creme fraiche in the cupboard. And I wouldn't have had a clue what to do with fennel, yams, mangoes or passion fruit - that is, if I could have found them. As for blueberries, maple syrup, waffles and muffins, well I would have been left wondering!

But things have certainly changed and today you can go shopping in your local supermarket for all sorts of exotic ingredients - it's as easy as American Pie!

A Few
Special Ingredients

YAMS

Yams are much larger than potatoes and have a woody, brown skin. They need to be well peeled to remove the tough outer layers and underneath you will find a dense, potato-texture that can be cooked by either boiling, baking or roasting.

SWEET POTATOES

Sweet potatoes are often confused with yams but they are a completely different item altogether. Their skin is normally much pinker than yams and not as tough. It is easy to see how they got their name though - they are noticeably sweeter than both traditional potatoes and yams.

BLUEBERRIES

These tiny, purple-blue, plump berries have a tart taste and can be found in shops from June through to August. Dried blueberries can now be bought and these work well in sauces and are good in muffin recipes. However, when it comes to pies, the flavour of the fresh berry is hard to beat.

OKRA

This unusual little vegetable is normally cut into chunks or slices and served as a traditional vegetable side dish. It is also used to thicken soups and stews because it somehow manages to become quite sticky when cooked. Okra is also known as lady's fingers or gumbo because its delicate shape resembles a lady's digits and because it is an essential ingredient if you are making an authentic gumbo stew.

MAPLE SYRUP

This is the processed sap of the maple tree and it has a very distinctive taste, though it is not so sweet as honey. It is often used as a topping for pancakes, waffles and ice cream and works as a wonderful marinade for baked ham.

A New England Chicken and Sweetcorn Chowder

A chowder is basically an American broth. This version is made with chicken, sweetcorn and vegetables and is so filling it can be served, not only as a soup but also as a tasty lunch dish.

570ml/1pt chicken stock
450g/1lb chicken pieces
1dssp oil
salt and pepper
115g/4oz bacon
2 onions, coarsely chopped
2 leek stalks
2 celery stalks
450g/1lb potatoes, peeled and diced
½tsp mixed herbs
570ml/1pt milk
1 red pepper, diced
2 large sweetcorn
70ml/⅛pt cream
2dssp parsley, finely chopped

Serves 6

Prepare the chicken stock in advance and keep it cool while the chowder is being prepared. Lightly fry the chicken pieces in a pan with 1dssp oil. Season with salt and pepper, cover with water and cook over a very low heat for 45 minutes or until cooked.

In a separate pan, fry the bacon for 5 minutes, then remove. Cook the onions, leeks and celery in the same pan for 5 minutes to slightly soften the vegetables. Add the potatoes, herbs, milk and chicken stock and simmer for 15 minutes. Do not allow the potatoes to soften too much. Add the bacon, the chicken pieces, peppers, sweetcorn, cream and parsley. Heat thoroughly and serve hot.

Louisiana Gumbo

Some people think of gumbo as a soup while others consider it a stew, but there is no denying that when it is served in the traditional way with cooked Patna (long-grain) rice, it is a very tasty and filling dish. One version of gumbo uses shellfish, but I prefer the more traditional, family-style dish made with broiled chicken and smoked ham.

ROUX:
2dssp oil
30g/1oz butter
30g/1oz flour

1 red pepper, diced
1 green pepper, diced
1 yellow pepper, diced
1 onion, chopped
1 courgette, diced
1 400g can chopped tomatoes
2 cloves garlic, chopped
1dssp light olive oil
680g/1½lb chicken pieces
850ml/1½pt water
1.1l/2pt chicken stock
340g/12oz smoked ham
4-5 okra, cut into 2.5cm/1inch pieces
½tsp mixed herbs
½tsp cayenne pepper

225g/8oz Patna rice
½tsp salt
boiling water to cook rice

Serves 6

Make the roux by heating the oil and butter in a large saucepan, then add the flour and blend together well. Cook over a gentle heat until the roux turns a nutty brown colour. (This should take several minutes depending upon the tem-

perature.) Add the diced peppers, chopped onion, courgettes, tinned tomatoes and garlic, and cook for a further 15 minutes. Be careful not to overcook the vegetables or the final appearance of the gumbo will be spoiled.

Heat the olive oil in another pan, add the chicken pieces, cook lightly, then add the water. Season and cover with lid. Cook very slowly for 1 hour. This is a very good way to cook meat as it retains all the succulence and flavour. Cook the ham pieces in the same way (or, if you prefer, use cooked ham instead). Add the chicken pieces, ham, chicken stock, okra, herbs and cayenne pepper to the vegetable mixture and heat through for 10 minutes.

While the gumbo is cooking, prepare the rice. Add the rice to boiling salted water in a large saucepan. Cook on a rapid boil for 8-10 minutes then drain.

Serve gumbo piping hot on a bed of cooked rice.

Baked Ballymoney Ham cooked the Virginia way

This rather unusual treatment of a ham works extremely well. The initial cooking in the oven, coupled with the marinade ensures a wonderfully succulent ham which is full of flavour.

8-9lbs unsmoked ham
1 onion, chopped
2 celery stalks, chopped
2 carrots, chopped
1.1l/2pt water

MARINADE:
140ml/¼pt maple syrup, heated
55g/2oz demerara sugar
3 cinnamon sticks

Serves 10-12

Place the ham in a large bowl, cover with cold water and leave to soak for at least 4 hours to remove excess salt. (Change the water several times during the process.) Dry the ham, then place in a foil lined roasting dish on top of the onions, celery and carrots. Pour the water over the top, close the foil securely around the ham and then place in a pre-heated oven at gas mark 3/160°C/350°F and bake (20-25 minutes per lb).

Approximately 30-45 minutes before the ham is cooked, take the ham out of the oven. Remove the rind and score the skin with a sharp knife. Place ham in the roasting tin on a clean piece of foil and pour over the marinade ingredients. Bake at gas mark 6/200°C/400°F with the foil open until the ham is caramelised and golden (approximately 30-45 minutes).

Creole of Vegetables

This creole is a tasty assortment of vegetables, and will add texture and flavour to any dish. The vegetables can be cooked separately and then combined with a spicy tomato sauce - this gives a better coloured dish.

SAUCE:
1dssp oil
2 cloves garlic, finely chopped
1 (400g) can chopped tomatoes
½tsp Cajun seasoning
½tsp cayenne pepper

CREOLE:
1dssp oil
1 green pepper, diced
2 stalks celery, chopped
1 onion, chopped
1 yellow courgette, chopped
1 green courgette, chopped

Serves 6

To prepare the sauce, heat the oil in a large frying pan and add the garlic. Cook for several minutes then add the tomatoes and continue to cook for several minutes. Then add seasoning.

In a separate pan prepare the creole. Heat the oil and add the pepper, celery, onion and courgettes. Cook over a high temperature for several minutes. Pour the sauce over the vegetables, place the lid on top and simmer over a low heat for 15 minutes. Serve hot.

A Knockout Carrot Cake

There are many varieties of carrot cake but this one is moist, spicy and terrific. The addition of crushed pineapple adds an extra touch of flavour to the cake.

3 eggs
115g/4oz caster sugar
55g/2oz butter, softened
70ml/⅛pt light vegetable oil
115g/4oz wholemeal flour
115g/4oz plain flour
1tsp baking soda
2tsp mixed spice
½tsp cinnamon
200g/7oz carrots, grated
115g/4oz sultanas
55g/2oz desiccated coconut
55g/2oz pecan nuts, finely chopped
1dssp crushed pineapple
rind of 1 orange

TOPPING:
55g/2oz butter, softened
225g/8oz full fat soft cheese or mascarpone cheese
85g/3oz icing sugar, sifted
few drops vanilla essence
55-85g/2-3oz pecan nuts
rind ½ orange

Makes 1 cake

Pre-heat oven to gas mark 4/180°C/350°F. Whisk the eggs and caster sugar together in a bowl until light and fluffy. Fold in the butter and oil and mix together lightly. In a separate bowl mix together the flours, baking soda, spice, carrots, sultanas, coconut, pecans, pineapple and orange rind. Add the egg mixture and mix well then transfer to a lined 900g/2lb loaf tin. Bake in the oven for 1-1¼ hours, until well risen and firm to the touch.

To make the icing, blend the butter and cream cheese together until smooth.

Add the icing sugar, vanilla and nuts and mix well. Spread the icing on top of the cake and decorate with whole pecan nuts and orange rind.

Baked Yams with Hazelnuts

Yams are similar in texture to potatoes and can be cooked and treated in much the same ways. When baked in the oven with nuts and a little oil, the flavour of the yam intensifies and tastes delicious.

3-4 yams
2dssp olive oil
30g/1oz demerara sugar
30g/1oz chopped hazelnuts
salt and pepper

Serves 4

Peel the woody bark from the yams, then cut into evenly sized wedges. Place in a roasting tin and sprinkle with oil, sugar, hazelnuts, salt and pepper. Roast, covered with foil, in the oven at gas mark 6/200°C/400°F for 1 hour. Remove the foil for the last 15 minutes to allow the dish to become golden and crispy. Serve hot.

Overleaf: A Knockout Carrot Cake (left) and Aunt Sally's Blueberry Waffles (right)

Aunt Sally's
Blueberry Waffles

My good friend, Aunt Sally, makes the best waffles I have ever tasted. They are so simple to make that I am amazed that they are not made at home more often. Buttermilk waffles are traditionally served with a warm blueberry sauce (see page 25) but also taste delicious when served with warm maple syrup or savoury-style with smoked bacon and sausage.

280ml/½pt water
85g/3oz fine oatmeal
55g/2oz butter, softened
2 eggs
280ml/½pt buttermilk
140g/5oz plain flour
pinch of salt
1tsp (heaped) baking powder
½tsp baking soda

Makes 8

Put the cold water and oatmeal into a saucepan. Bring to boiling point, stirring all the time, until the mixture thickens. Remove from the heat, add the softened butter and mix well. Leave to cool.

Mix the eggs and buttermilk together, then fold them into the oatmeal mixture. Oil and preheat the waffle iron. In a separate bowl, sieve the flour, salt and raising agents together, then add the liquid mixture, stirring as it goes in but being careful not to over-mix. I find it easier to put the mixture into a jug before pouring it into the waffle iron. Cook for 3 minutes on either side then turn out and serve hot.

Blueberry
Sauce

Although tiny, blueberries are just full of flavour - tangy, tart and refreshing. I try to use fresh berries whenever I can, but dried blueberries work well in this recipe.

4dssp blueberry jam
1dssp water
pinch powdered cinnamon
30g/1oz dried or fresh blueberries

Serves 8

Heat all the ingredients together in a saucepan for 1 minute. Allow to cool slightly before serving with fresh, warm blueberry waffles (see page 24), and a scoop of vanilla ice cream.

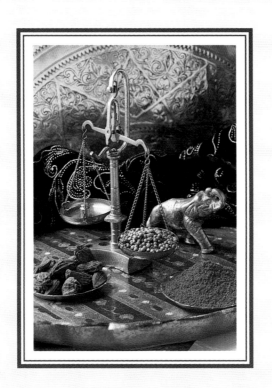

Indian Spice

I f I was to mention turmeric, chillies, ginger, dates, figs, saffron and rice - you would most likely know I was talking about primary ingredients in Indian cooking. Luckily the spices and flavours of India are readily available in our supermarkets so we can all put a little Indian spice into our everyday cooking.

A Few
Special Ingredients

TURMERIC
A wonderful, brilliant yellow, ground spice used more for its colour than its flavour. Be careful when using it as it will stain your hands and clothes and is very difficult to remove.

FRESH FIGS
When ripe, figs should be soft to the touch with a sweet, sap-like smell. If they have even the slightest hint of sourness, don't buy them. Figs don't keep very well, so they should be stored in the refrigerator until used. They taste really good when poached with apricots or served with a little honey over the top.

GINGER
Ginger comes from the root of the ginger plant and is one of the most popular spices. It can be used either fresh, dried, pickled or powdered and has a lovely lemony smell. It is best used as fresh as possible and is a vital ingredient in Indian and Chinese cuisine. I love the flavour of freshly grated root ginger, spring onion and garlic cooked together in a little olive oil - it is an ideal base for stir-fry recipes. Look out for the many other forms of ginger; crystallised and preserved root ginger in syrup work beautifully in sauces and meringues.

GARAM MASALA
Garam means 'hot' and *Masala* means 'spicy' and when combined together they are wonderfully aromatic. The blend is basically a combination of cardamom seeds, whole cloves, black peppercorns, cumin seeds, cinnamon sticks and nutmeg, though everyone has their own particular recipe and the quantites of each spice used can vary considerably. The spices are blended together, pounded or turned into a paste by adding a small onion, lightly cooked in olive oil, to the dried spices and then blending in a small food processor. I find it best to add Garam Masala at the end of a recipe so that it retains its heat and flavour.

Creamy Chicken and Pear Curry

The best known dish of India must surely be the curry, from the hottest of them all, the Vindaloo, to the milder Tikka. There are hundreds of spice combinations and flavours, and just as many methods to make curry. This mild, creamy recipe is a gentle introduction to curries, though it is not a traditional Indian dish.

4dssp lemon juice
1dssp nut flavoured oil
salt and pepper
680g/1½lb chicken pieces
oil to fry

SAUCE:
1dssp oil
1 onion
1 cooking apple, diced
2 pears, sliced
50g/2oz sultanas
4dssp mango chutney
1dssp tomato puree
2dssp tikka paste
280ml/½pt vegetable stock
140ml/¼pt coconut milk

Serves 4

Mix the lemon juice, oil and seasoning together. Cut the chicken into bite-size pieces and add to the marinade. Allow to stand for at least 15 minutes. After marinating, remove the chicken pieces and fry them in oil for 5 minutes to seal in the juices.

In a separate pan make the sauce. Heat the oil and lightly fry the onion, apple and pears for 2 minutes until softened. Add the sultanas, mango chutney, tomato puree and tikka paste and stir well. Add the lightly cooked chicken pieces, the stock and coconut milk. Bring to simmering point and cook gently for 20-25 minutes.

Serve with either plain or Saffron Rice (see page 40).

Loin of Pork with Whole Spices and Ginger Marmalade

Ginger and coriander are two popular Indian spices and they combine well with most meats. In this dish I use them with a roast loin of pork, and I find the aromatic flavours develop wonderfully. I have used coriander seeds in the recipes as I find their flavour is more pungent than coriander powder. Do not substitute coriander leaves in this dish as the flavour is entirely different!

1.8kg/4lb loin of pork
115g/4oz ginger marmalade
2dssp coriander seeds, crushed
2 inch (5cm) root ginger, cut into pieces
salt and pepper
280ml/½pt vegetable stock
1dssp nut flavoured oil

Serves 8

Preheat oven to gas mark 5/190°C/375°F. Remove the rind from the pork and score the fat at intervals with a sharp knife to allow the spices to penetrate further into the pork. Spread the loin with 1dssp of ginger marmalade to help the crushed seeds stick to the sides, then sprinkle over the seeds. Transfer to a foil-lined dish, sprinkle a few pieces of root ginger around the pork and season. Pour in the stock and oil and close the foil loosely over the pork. Roast in the oven for 30-35 minutes per lb plus an extra 30 minutes at the end of the cooking time, if you like your pork well cooked. Approximately 45 minutes before the pork is cooked, open the foil and pour the remaining marmalade over the top of the roast. Return to the oven, uncovered, and cook until the marmalade bubbles and gives the pork a wonderful, crunchy topping. Cut into slices and serve hot.

Cauliflower and Broccoli with a Hint of the Orient

This is a clever way to liven up ordinary broccoli and cauliflower. It is surprising how popular these vegetables are when cooked with spices and given a hint of the Orient.

½ head cauliflower florets
1 bunch broccoli florets
1 dssp nut oil
1 clove garlic, chopped finely
1 inch (2.5cm) root ginger
1 dssp brown mustard seeds
1 dssp balsamic vinegar

Serves 4

Blanch the cauliflower and broccoli florets in boiling water for 1 minute to improve their colour and shorten the cooking time. The secret in cooking vegetables for this dish is to retain their crunchy flavour.

Heat the oil in a frying pan and add the garlic, ginger and mustard seeds (these will pop open and release their nutty flavour). Then add the blanched vegetables and toss around for a couple of minutes. Add the vinegar and serve hot on a platter.

Gingered Carrots and Parsnips

Carrots and parsnips are a wonderful combination of vegetables. When treated in this way with ginger, sesame oil and honey they become very aromatic but retain their characteristic flavours which marry so well together.

3 carrots, cut into fine matchsticks
3 parsnips, cut into fine matchsticks
1dssp sesame oil
1 inch (2.5cm) root ginger
1tsp honey
1tsp sesame seeds

Serves 4

Steam the carrots and parsnips for 2-3 minutes. Heat the oil in a frying pan and add the ginger and honey. Heat through before adding the steamed vegetables. Toss for 1 minute then and add a sprinkling of sesame seeds over the top. Serve hot.

Indian Turmeric Spiced Chicken

It's the turmeric that gives this dish such a vibrant colour. After the stock has been added to this dish it can either be simmered on the hob or cooked in the oven at gas mark 6/200°C/400°F for 45minutes.

1tsp turmeric
½tsp chilli flakes
1 small red chilli, chopped
1 clove garlic, chopped
1 stick cinnamon
55g/2oz almond, pistachio or pine nuts
55g/2oz sultanas
4dssp olive oil
2dssp lemon juice
½tsp salt
680g/1½lb chicken joints (legs, drumsticks and wings)
1dssp olive oil
280ml/½pt chicken or vegetable stock

Serves 4

Prepare the marinade by mixing the turmeric, chilli, garlic, cinnamon, nuts, sultanas, oil, lemon juice and salt together in a bowl. Stir well and pour over the chicken pieces, then leave to marinate for 1 hour in a covered dish.

After marinating, remove the chicken pieces and fry them gently in the oil. Cook on either side until golden, then add the marinade and the vegetable stock. Replace the lid and leave to simmer gently for 30 minutes or until the chicken pieces are tender and falling off the bone. The stock can be thickened, if desired, by adding ½dssp of cornflour blended in a little water. This dish is very simple to cook and the colour will be wonderful thanks to the golden turmeric.

Serve with Jewelled Rice (see page 36) and Spiced Oranges (see page 37).

Indian Turmeric Spiced Chicken

Jewelled Rice

Plain boiled rice can be one of the most difficult ingredients to cook, but over the years I've learned to buy a good brand of rice, make sure I wash it well before cooking and keep the rice on a rapid boil throughout the cooking.

450g/1lb rice
1dssp nut oil
15g/½oz butter
55g/2oz golden raisins
30g/1oz almonds or pistachios
2dssp parsley, finely chopped

Serves 4

Cook the long grain rice in boiling, salted water until all the liquid has absorbed (approximately 10 minutes), then keep warm.

In a separate pan heat the oil and butter, then stir in the raisins, nuts and parsley. Add to the rice and mix lightly, before serving.

Spiced Oranges

Sliced, fresh fruit is often served as a refreshing accompaniment with Indian food. The fruit can be spiced with cloves, cinnamon or coriander and, to add extra flavour, either a little oil, honey or balsamic vinegar sprinkled over the top. Choose whichever combination you prefer.

4 oranges, peeled and cut into slices
2tsp light oil, honey or balsamic vinegar
¼tsp spice (cloves, cinnamon or coriander)

Serves 4

Remove the rind and pith from the oranges then slice as finely as possible. Arrange in a serving dish, sprinkle with the oil and cinnamon, then serve chilled.

Homemade Garam Masala Paste

1 onion, finely chopped
2dssp oil
1dssp cardamom seeds
1tssp clove powder
1tsp black peppercorns
1tsp cumin seeds
1 stick cinnamon
1tsp coriander powder
1tsp chilli powder

Lightly cook the onion in oil, then transfer to a blender with the cardamom seeds, clove powder, peppercorns, cumin seeds and cinnamon stick. Blend until the mixture forms a smooth paste, then add the coriander and chilli powders and mix well. The heat and strength of this homemade Garam Masala paste can easily be varied by adjusting the quantities of chilli and cardamom.

Saffron Rice

This subtly-flavoured rice is made with Basmati, the finest of all Indian rices. It is good with any curry but especially great with my Creamy Chicken and Pear Curry (see page 29).

450g/1lb Basmati rice
1tsp light oil
15g/½oz butter
1 small onion, finely chopped
½tsp saffron threads, crushed to a powder
570ml/1pt light chicken stock or boiling water

Serves 4

Wash the rice and dry thoroughly. Heat the oil and butter in a saucepan and cook the onion for 1 minute. Add the saffron and stir. Pour in the rice and stir until all the grains are well coated, then add the boiling stock or water. Stir once and leave to simmer for 10-12 minutes until all the liquid has been absorbed. Do not be tempted to stir the rice during cooking or it will become sticky. Transfer to a serving bowl and serve hot.

Roasted Pears with Spiced Yoghurt

A simple pudding of fresh fruit poached whole or roasted in the oven. Indian puddings are often simple: just some fresh fruit enhanced with a touch of spice. The juice which the fruit cooks in forms the basis of the syrup which flavours the yoghurt – a fresh-tasting accompaniment to the pears.

115g/4oz Greek yoghurt
8 pears
140ml/¼pt water
1 lemon, rind and juice
2-3dssp honey or maple syrup
6-8 cloves, juniper berries or ½ inch (1cm) root ginger
30g/1oz flaked almonds

SAUCE:
30g/1oz granulated sugar
70ml/⅛pt syrup from cooked pears

Serves 4

Choose good firm pears for this pudding, then cut a slice from the bottom of each so they can sit steadily. Scoop out the seeds from the centre of the pears then place them upright (lightly packed together) in an ovenproof dish. Pour in the water, lemon juice and rind, honey or maple syrup and finally the spice.

Bake in the oven at gas mark 5/190°C/375°F for 15-20 minutes until pears are soft but still retain their shape. Remove the pears and transfer to a serving dish. Strain half the syrup into a saucepan and add the sugar. Bring to a boil until the syrup is reduced by half. Allow to cool, then use to flavour the natural yoghurt. Serve with the cooked pears.

Ginger Meringue
with Fresh Figs

Stem ginger and brown sugar work a treat in a typical meringue: the ginger gives it such flavour and the brown sugar a crunchiness and light golden colour. Topped with yoghurt, pistachio nuts and a rich chocolate sauce (see page 44), this pudding is a delight for those with a sweet tooth!

4 egg whites
170g/6oz caster sugar
55g/2oz soft brown sugar
55g/2oz stem ginger, finely chopped
140ml/¼pt whipped cream
140ml/¼pt yoghurt
rind ½ lemon
30g/1oz nuts, chopped
6 fresh figs or kiwi fruit, sliced

Preheat oven to gas mark 1/140°C/275°F. First make the meringue: beat together the egg whites with 4oz caster sugar until stiff and forming peaks, then fold in the remaining caster sugar and soft brown sugar. Fold in the stem ginger, then transfer to a greased sheet of paper and shape into a round. Bake in the oven for 1 hour. When cooked, turn off the oven and leave the meringue to cool in the oven before decorating.

Mix together the lightly whipped cream and yoghurt, add the lemon rind and nuts. Mix together well, then spoon over the meringue and decorate with the figs or kiwi fruit slices.

Ginger Meringue with Fresh Figs and a Bitter Chocolate Sauce

Bitter Chocolate Sauce

This decadent rich dark chocolate sauce combines well with ice cream, fresh fruit or steamed puddings. I like to serve it drizzled over the Ginger Meringue with Fresh Figs (see page 43).

70ml/⅛pt milk
70ml/⅛pt cream
115g/4oz chocolate

Serves 6

Heat the milk and cream over a low heat but do not allow to boil. Add the chocolate a little at a time until it melts and the sauce has thickened. Serve at once drizzled over the meringue.

A Few
Special Ingredients

GREEK YOGHURT
The thick, creamy texture, consistency and slightly acidic flavour of this yoghurt make it very versatile. Used on its own, as a replacement for whipped cream, it makes a less-calorific topping, or mixed with cream it will help the cream keep better in warm conditions. It is usually made from cow's milk and the fat content varies.

AUBERGINES
The most common variety of aubergine in our greengrocers is the deep purple, egg-shaped type. The skin is smooth, glossy and delicate and, when fresh, the flesh is sweet. If your aubergines are a little bitter, salting the slices will help remove the tartness. Although aubergines look sturdy, they do not store very well, so eat within one week of buying in order to enjoy them at their best. When buying aubergines, try to pick ones which are firm, but avoid soft aubergines - a sure sign they are old - or hard aubergines - they will be under-ripe.

FETA CHEESE
A few cubes of this cheese adds a special Greek touch to an ordinary salad. It looks like quite a firm cheese yet it crumbles very easily. It has a salty flavour when eaten uncooked in salads, yet, when lightly cooked it loses this saltiness. It has a unique flavour and is made from ewe's milk, although Danish Feta is often made from cow's milk. Both are a brilliant white colour.

Glorious Food
from Greece

For me the most valuable food to come from Greece must be their velvety-textured yoghurt, their fruit and, of course, aubergines. And now that these foods are available to us all year round, we don't have to wait for that summer holiday to enjoy glorious food from Greece.

Chicken cooked the Aegean Way with a Walnut Sauce

It is always good to discover a new chicken recipe and this is one of the best I've tried. Walnuts are used often in Greek cookery, and their flavour changes totally when cooked. Using walnut powder to thicken a sauce is an very old idea - it dates back to the Persians! I use a mortar and pestle to grind fresh walnuts, and I usually leave them a little coarse as I find this adds more texture to the dish.

30g/1oz plain flour
salt and pepper
4 chicken fillets
2dssp olive oil
30g/1oz butter
70ml/⅛pt white wine
280ml/½pt vegetable stock
55g/2oz walnuts, ground
2inch (5cm) strip leeks, shredded finely
½ lemon rind and juice
2dssp cream
1dssp parsley, finely chopped
a few halved walnuts to decorate

Serves 4

Mix the flour, salt and pepper together and use to coat the chicken fillets. Heat the oil and butter in a frying pan then add the chicken fillets and cook for several minutes on either side. Add the wine and vegetable stock and simmer very slowly for 1 hour until the chicken is cooked and the liquid becomes syrupy. Add the ground walnuts, leeks, lemon rind and juice, cream and parsley. Stir in and cook for several minutes, then serve.

Scatter a few halved walnuts on top of the dish just before serving.

My
Moussaka

Moussaka is to the Greeks what cottage pie is to us - a wholesome family meal. Indeed even the ingredients are similar; both are based on minced lamb and potato. However, the addition of red wine, aubergines and herbs makes these basic ingredients into a very tasty dish.

2 aubergines, cut into 1cm slices
3 or 4 potatoes, peeled and cut into 1cm slices
1dssp olive oil
3 cloves garlic
1 large onion, coarsely chopped
450g/1lb minced lamb
salt and pepper
¼tsp cayenne pepper
2tbsp tomato puree
2 or 3 tomatoes, diced
1tsp oregano (fresh or dried)
2tsp parsley, finely chopped
140ml/¼pt red wine
140ml/¼pt vegetable stock (if you are not using wine
use double the amount of stock, i.e. 280ml/½pt)
225g/8oz Greek yoghurt
2 egg yolks
115g/4oz grated cheese (Mozzarella or Gruyere)

Serves 6-8

Prepare the aubergines by removing the stalks, then cut into slices and sprinkle with salt. Set aside for 30 minutes to allow the salt to remove the bitter juices. Rinse aubergine slices, then place in a steamer and cook for 2-3 minutes. Peel and slice the potatoes into rounds half an inch (1cm) thick and steam for 5 minutes until slightly softened.

Preheat oven to gas mark 5/190°C/375°F. Heat the olive oil in a large frying pan, add the garlic and onion and cook over a high temperature. Add the minced lamb and cook until browned. Add the salt, pepper, cayenne pepper, tomato puree, diced tomatoes, oregano and parsley. Mix well, then add the wine (if using) and stock. Cook until the liquid reduces, then begin to assemble

the moussaka.

In an ovenproof dish, layer the potatoes, half the aubergines, the lamb mixture and finally another layer of aubergines. Mix the Greek yoghurt, egg yolks, half the grated cheese, salt and pepper together. Spread this over the moussaka, then sprinkle with the remaining cheese and dust with cayenne pepper. Bake in the oven for 45-50 minutes.

Greek Country Salad

A tasty colourful salad which is usually made with feta cheese with its salty, slightly sour flavour.

4 plum tomatoes, sliced
1 red onion, cut into slices
8-10 black olives
115g/4oz feta cheese

DRESSING:
2dssp olive oil
1dssp balsamic vinegar
salt and pepper

TO SERVE:
shredded basil leaves
pinch cayenne pepper

Arrange the sliced tomatoes, onions, olives and feta cheese in a dish. Prepare the dressing by mixing together the oil, vinegar and seasoning. Pour over the salad and garnish with basil and cayenne pepper.

Deep-fried Aubergine Crisps with Tzatziki

Home-made vegetable crisps are delicious and none are better than those made with aubergines. Served with a tangy tzatziki dip they are great for a party.

2-3 aubergines, cut into fine slices
oil to deep fat fry

TZATZIKI:
2tbsp olive oil
1tsp white vinegar
1 clove garlic, peeled and crushed
225g/8oz plain thick yoghurt or Greek yoghurt
salt and pepper to taste
½ cucumber, peeled and grated coarsely
2tbsp fresh mint, chopped

Cut the aubergines into wafer thin slices, then fry in hot oil until crispy and golden. Blot on kitchen paper and serve.

Prepare the tzatziki by beating the oil, vinegar and garlic together in a bowl, using a fork. Add the yoghurt, salt and pepper and beat lightly until well blended and smooth. Squeeze as much liquid out of the grated cucumber as you can, then add the cucumber flesh and the mint and stir well. Chill the dip in the refrigerator before serving.

Pan-fried Mullet
with a Grape Sauce

An old proverb advised that 'best fish is fresh fish', and I certainly agree with it! I am also a great believer that a fish such as red mullet is best if cooked simply. Take time to scale this fish properly, as the scales are firm and do not soften with cooking.

2 red mullet, boned and scaled
1dssp olive oil
30g/1oz butter
1dssp lemon juice
pinch salt

SAUCE:
1dssp olive oil
1 spring onion, finely chopped
55g/2oz green grapes
55g/2oz black grapes
1tsp white wine or balsamic vinegar
1dssp honey or 30g/1oz demerara sugar
1dssp parsley, finely chopped

Serves 2

Clean and scale the fish, then pat dry. Fry in the hot oil and butter for 2 minutes on either side. Sprinkle a little lemon juice over the top, then season with salt and keep warm.

To make the sauce, heat the oil and fry the spring onions until just opaque. Add the grapes, white wine or vinegar, honey and parsley. Bring to a boil then serve straight away poured over the mullet. Be careful not to overcook this sauce or the colour of the grapes will be spoiled.

Oven Baked
Potatoes with Chives

I increasingly find myself using the most simple and trouble-free methods of cooking vegetables. This must surely be one of the easiest and most effective ways to cook potatoes, yet the flavour and food value is excellent. Substitute the chives with rosemary or parsley, if you prefer.

4-5 potatoes
1/4 onion, finely chopped
1dssp chives, chopped
425ml/³⁄₄pt milk or cream
pinch of salt

Serves 4

Preheat oven to gas mark 6/200°C/400°F. Cut the peeled potatoes into fine slices and arrange half of them in a well oiled ovenproof dish. Sprinkle with half the chopped onion and chives, then arrange the second layer of potatoes and sprinkle with the remaining onions and chives. Pour over the milk or cream, cover with foil and bake in the oven for 35-45 minutes. The cooking time will vary depending upon the thickness of the potatoes but, I find, the thinner the potatoes the nicer the dish.

My Greek Tart with a Lemony Syrup Sauce

This is my version of Greek baklava. It is not just as sweet as the traditional dessert as I use honey as a substitute for sugar. Serve either with the lemon sauce or Greek yoghurt, or just on its own.

4 sheets filo pastry
1dssp honey
15g/½oz butter
225g/8oz sultanas
55g/2oz hazelnuts
pinch cinnamon
2dssp lemon juice
2dssp sherry

SAUCE:
juice of 2 lemons
rind of ½ lemon
2dssp honey
30g/1oz soft brown sugar
1 stick cinnamon

Serves 8

Preheat oven to gas mark 6/200°C/400°F. Layer the pastry sheets onto a flat board and brush each with melted butter. Arrange the sheets in a lightly greased 6-7 inch (15-16cm) cake tin, and ensure the edges overhang the rim of the tin, as they will be used to cover the filling.

Prepare the filling by melting the honey and butter together in a saucepan. Add the sultanas, hazelnuts, cinnamon, lemon and sherry. Stir well and leave to infuse for 10 minutes before spooning into the filo pastry case. Carefully fold the overhanging edges of pastry over the filling, brush with melted butter and bake in the oven for 8-10 minutes.

To make the sauce, put the honey, lemon juice, peel and cinnamon stick into a saucepan and heat gently. Cook for 5 minutes until bubbling and slightly thickened. Remove the cinnamon stick, and serve drizzled over the fruit tart.

Aubergines with Crispy Bacon and Cheese

Aubergines have so many uses; either as a vegetable side dish, a main ingredient in Moussaka, or the basis of a simple little starter. Here I have topped them with goat's cheese, sun-dried tomatoes, olive oil and bacon, and they taste delicious.

1 aubergine, sliced lengthways
2tsp sun-dried tomato paste
55g/2oz goat's cheese or Mozzarella, cut into rounds
1dssp walnut oil
black pepper
2 rashers streaky bacon, cut into strips

Serves 2

Sprinkle the aubergine slices with salt, and set aside for 30 minutes to allow the bitter juices to run off. Rinse each slice with water and pat dry.

Grill for 1-2 minutes on each side, then blot on kitchen paper. Place a teaspoon of sun-dried tomato paste on top of each slice aubergine, top with a round of cheese, sprinkle with oil and black pepper then grill for 2-3 minutes. Serve hot garnished with bacon strips.

A Very Berry Greek Pudding

Greek yoghurt and berry puddings are simply perfect together, and the flavours and textures contrast so beautifully. Don't worry if you can't get the fruits I have used - this pudding can be made with whatever fruits are in season; in autumn I use lightly poached apples, plums and blackberries.

FILLING:
450g/1lb soft berry fruits (e.g. strawberries, raspberries, currants, blueberries)
30g/1oz demerara sugar

TOPPING:
225g/8oz Greek yoghurt (or 115g/4oz fromage frais and
115g/4oz Greek yoghurt combined)
30g/1oz icing sugar
2 passionfruits, juice and seeds
a few sprigs of mint

Makes 1 pudding

Wash and dry the fruits, toss together in a serving bowl, then sprinkle with demerara sugar. Prepare the topping by mixing together the yoghurt, fromage frais (or/and yoghurt mixture), icing sugar, half the passion fruit seeds and a quarter of the berries. Pour the yoghurt mixture over the berries in the serving bowl, then sprinkle with demerara sugar and the remaining passionfruit seeds. Serve decorated with a sprig of mint.

The Italian Influence

I f I were to ask you what we have gained from Italian cookery you would, most likely, reel off a list that includes pasta, olive oil, balsamic vinegar, cheeses and breads. And you'd be right! These wonderful ingredients are fast becoming as popular as our own home-grown carrots, parsnips and potatoes, and our supermarkets offer a fabulous range of Italian produce. Personally, though, I would have to say that our greatest influence isn't the produce itself, but rather Italy's wholesome, family-orientated way of cooking - an approach we can easily identify with.

A Few
Special Ingredients

MASCARPONE CHEESE

Rich, thick, creamy and so versatile, Mascarpone cheese has so many uses. It is wonderful added to stock to make a creamy sauce for fish or chicken, as a topping or filling for cakes, or combined with poached or fresh fruit. It does have a high fat content (similar to whipping cream), but as it blends well with low-fat yoghurt or fromage frais, it is easy to make it less-calorific and more healthy.

BALSAMIC VINEGAR

This is surely one of the greatest vinegars ever to come out of Italy. It has such a rich, sweet, yet mellow, flavour and can be used in a variety of ways. It can bring out the best flavour in strawberries (try sprinkling them with a teaspoonful), spruce up salad dressings or add life to sauces. There are many varieties and different brands; but my advice is to invest in a good balsalmic vinegar - it will keep better and last longer.

PARMESAN CHEESE

This must be the real 'soul' of Italian cooking: it adds such flavour and style to even the simplest of dishes. Made from cow's milk, Parmesan has a sweet, nutty taste and a grainy texture. It can be grated and added at the table or used during cooking in a variety of traditional Italian dishes.

OLIVE OIL

Now available in many forms - light, pure, virgin, extra virgin - which can be confusing. The best olive oil comes from the first pressing of the olives and is known as extra virgin oil. It has a pure and delicate flavour and is good for raw salad dressings, salsas and sauces. However, cooking extra virgin oil spoils its superior flavour and so it is best to use a less expensive type if you plan to heat the oil.

MOZZARELLA CHEESE

There are two main types of Mozzarella: one made from cow's milk and one from buffalo milk. Buffalo milk Mozzarella is the authentic one and is ideal eaten sliced, on its own and raw. Cow's milk Mozzarella is best for cooking and very good in sauces as it has a mild, creamy flavour. It is widely used in pizzas, lasagnes and as a topping for quick snacks.

Cod cooked the Sicilian way with Black Olives and Parmesan

This is such a tasty way to liven up a fillet of cod. This recipe can also be made with hake, whiting or your favourite white fish.

2 cod fillets
salt and pepper
1dssp oil
2dssp olive paste (a sun-dried tomato paste)

CRUST:
55g/2oz brown breadcrumbs
1dssp parsley, finely chopped
½ lemon rind and juice
55g/2oz parmesan cheese, grated
2dssp olive oil

Serves 2

Preheat oven to gas mark 5/190°C/375°F. Remove the bones from the cod fillets and place them on a lightly oiled baking sheet. Sprinkle with salt, pepper and a little oil, then spread the olive paste on top.

Prepare the crust by mixing the breadcrumbs and parsley together and then adding the lemon rind and juice, parmesan cheese and oil to form a paste. Carefully spread over the top and pat down well. Place in the oven and bake for approximately 25 minutes. (Cooking time will vary depending on the thickness of the fish fillets.)

Serve hot with Champ (see page 68) and a Salsa of Tomato and Avocado (see page 69).

Parsley Soup

For years I've been using parsley just as a garnish, but by chance one day I discovered it makes one of the tastiest soups I've ever tasted, with a wonderfully vivid colour and distinctive flavour.

1dssp light oil
2 leeks, sliced (white part only)
2 potatoes, finely diced
2 cups parsley heads
1.1l/2pt chicken stock
salt and pepper

TO SERVE:
2 pieces of bacon, grilled and cut into strips
swirl of cream

Serves 6

Heat the oil in a large saucepan, add the leeks and potatoes and sweat them for 5 minutes. Add 1 cup of parsley along with the stock and seasoning. Bring to the boil then simmer gently for 15 minutes. Add the remaining parsley and cook for no longer than 2 minutes. Pour the soup into a blender and process until smooth. Return the soup to the saucepan and reheat but do not boil.

Serve warm with bacon strips and a swirl of cream on top.

Champ

Like every classic dish, there is a 'knack' to getting the best flavour out of the simplest ingredients.

680g/1½lb floury potatoes
570ml/1pt milk
30g/1oz butter (or polyunsaturated fat)
2dssp spring onions, very finely chopped
salt and pepper

Serves 6

Cook the potatoes in a pot of boiling salted water until soft, then drain and mash finely.

In a separate pan, heat together the milk, butter, spring onions and seasoning until the butter melts. Pour over the hot potatoes, mix lightly together but do not overbeat or you will spoil the floury texture of the potatoes and the colour of the spring onions. Serve piping hot.

A Salsa of
Tomato and Avocado

A salsa is simply a 'sal' or chopped up relish, which combines a dressing with evenly diced vegetables and fruits. The colours in this one are particularly good: the red tomatoes and green avocados look very appetising.

4 tomatoes skinned, de-seeded and diced
1 avocado, peeled, stoned and diced
1tsp spring onion, finely chopped
¼tsp red chilli, finely chopped
¼tsp green chilli, finely chopped
1tsp basil, finely shredded

DRESSING:
3dssp olive oil
1dssp rice wine vinegar
pinch mustard
pinch caster sugar
salt and pepper

Serves 6

Mix the vegetables together and put into a serving bowl. To make the dressing, mix together the oil, vinegar, mustard, sugar and seasoning. Add the dressing to the diced tomatoes mixture and mix together very lightly. Serve at once, garnished with finely shredded basil leaves and a sprinkling of spring onions.

Chicken Italiana

This combination of chicken, balsamic vinegar, a rich creamy mascarpone cheese sauce and a hint of mushroom works so well. The dish can be prepared in advance but be careful not to overheat the sauce otherwise it may become runny. An alternative topping for this dish is toasted breadcrumbs or couscous.

4 chicken fillets
4dssp balsamic vinegar
2dssp olive oil
2 cloves garlic, finely chopped
340g/12oz mushrooms, finely sliced
15g/½oz butter (or polyunsaturated fat)
4dssp parsley, finely chopped

SAUCE:
295g/1 tin condensed chicken or mushroom soup
250g/1 tub mascarpone cheese
140ml/¼pt chicken stock

BRUSCHETTA TOPPING:
1 baguette, sliced and toasted
1 clove garlic, finely chopped
70ml/⅛pt olive oil

Serves 6

Preheat oven to gas mark 5/190°C/375°F. Cut the chicken fillets into evenly sized pieces and toss in the balsamic vinegar. This will give the chicken a golden colour and rich musky flavour. Heat 1dssp of oil in a pan, add the garlic and cook for 5-6 minutes. In a separate pan cook the finely sliced mushrooms in the butter and remaining oil for several minutes being careful not to overcook. Layer the chicken pieces and lightly cooked mushrooms in an ovenproof dish and sprinkle generously with parsley.

In a separate pan heat the soup, cheese and chicken stock, but do not allow to boil. Add a little water to the sauce until its consistency resembles double cream, then pour over the chicken pieces and mushrooms.

To prepare the topping, cut the bread into angular slices and toast until golden brown on both sides. Rub the bread with garlic, pour over a little oil, and arrange the slices in an overlapping fashion on top of the sauce. If liked, freshly grated cheese can be sprinkled over the bread before placing the dish in the oven. Bake for 30-35 minutes and serve hot.

A Warm Roasted
Red Pepper Dressing

This is a great dressing for a classic green salad. A strong flavoured oil will swamp the subtle taste of this dressing so, for best results, a light oil is essential. The dressing can be served warm or cold, although I find the flavour intensifies greatly when it is reheated.

1 red pepper, roasted and softened
140ml/¼pt light oil (e.g. grapeseed oil)
1dssp rice wine vinegar
pinch salt and pepper
pinch chilli powder

Makes 140ml/¼pt

Cut the pepper in half and remove the seeds. Roast the pepper in a hot oven or under the grill until soft. Then peel the skin off and discard it. Blend the pepper flesh until soft, but be careful not to over blend or the final colour of the sauce will be affected. Add the oil, vinegar, seasoning and chilli powder to the pepper and blend again for a few seconds. Serve either cold or lightly warmed. (Do not serve the dressing too hot or the salad will spoil).

Rich Dark Espresso Sauce

This sauce is excellent served over the top of vanilla ice cream and decorated with coarsely flaked almonds, chocolate curls and fresh cherries.

55g/2oz butter
85g/3oz soft brown sugar
1 egg yolk
6tbsp whipped cream
3tbsp freshly made espresso coffee

Makes 140ml/¼pt

Melt the butter and soft brown sugar together over a low heat, then add the egg yolk and mix well. Add the cream and heat until the sauce thickens. Finally, fold in the coffee, heat thoroughly and serve.

Soda Bread Pizza

I find this base is much simpler than the traditional, time-consuming ones containing yeast. The combination of water and milk, either low-fat or full cream, to mix the dry ingredients works well when combined with olive oil.

170g/6oz soda bread flour
pinch of salt
2dssp olive oil
70ml/⅛pt water
70ml/⅛ milk
2dssp tinned tomatoes, finely chopped (or tomato paste)

TOPPING:
2 cloves garlic
1 red onion, coarsely chopped
225g/8oz mildly cured bacon, chopped into large pieces
4 tomatoes, coarsely chopped
½tsp oregano
1dssp olive oil
115g/4oz mozzarella cheese, sliced
8-10 black olives

Makes 1 pizza

Preheat oven to gas mark 5/190°C/375°F. Sieve the flour into a bowl, then add the salt, olive oil, water and milk. Blend together well to form a soft dough. Turn out on to a floured table and knead lightly before shaping into a round, flat pancake approximately 9-10 inches (22-25cm) in diameter. Place on a lightly floured baking sheet and brush with a little olive oil. This will help to firm the dough during cooking and will also prevent the base becoming soggy when the topping is added. Spread the tomatoes or tomato paste evenly over the top of the base.

Prepare the topping by gently frying the garlic, onion, bacon, tomatoes and oregano in the oil. Cook for 1-2 minutes - just long enough to allow the flavours to combine - then spread on top of the pizza base. Garnish with slices of mozzarella cheese and black olives then cook in the oven for 20-25 minutes until golden, firm and well cooked. Serve either hot or cold.

A Peach of an Almond and Amaretto Pie

This tasty pie has a most unusual crumbly base and a short cooking time. The flavour of amaretto in the biscuits, combined with the peaches gives a subtle, but stunning, taste.

140g/5oz oatmeal
45g/1½oz amaretto biscuits, crushed
30g/1oz ground almonds
30g/1oz soft brown sugar
70g/2½oz butter, softened

TOPPING:
2 tins peaches
30g/1oz melted butter
2dssp honey
30g/1oz demerara sugar
55g/2oz crumbled amaretto biscuits

Makes 1 pie

Preheat oven to gas mark 6/200°C/400°F. Grease a 9 inch (22cm) loose bottomed flan tin. Mix the oatmeal, biscuit crumbs, almonds and sugar together in a bowl. Add the butter and stir in until the mixture has a crumbly consistency. Pour mixture into the flan tin and press down firmly.

Drain the peaches and arrange on the base. Drizzle the melted butter and honey over the peaches, then dust with demerara sugar and amaretto biscuits before placing in the oven. Bake for 15-20 minutes until well cooked and golden on top.

Amaretto Custard

Be careful not to let this sauce boil or the texture will be totally spoiled (and you may need a sieve to remove the lumps!).

280ml/½pt milk and 15g/½oz cornflour, blended
3 egg yolks, lightly beaten
15g/½oz caster sugar
few drops vanilla essence
2dssp amaretto liqueur

Serves 4-6

Heat the milk and cornflour in a saucepan. Add the egg yolks and sugar, and beat gently, over a low heat, until the custard shows signs of thickening. Add the vanilla essence and amaretto liqueur and stir. Serve immediately.

A Feast from the East

Chinese food is renowned all over the world and we only have to look at the number of restaurants and take-aways in our towns to see just how popular it is. Thanks to the improved availability of items such as sauces, noodles, rice, seasonings and, of course, woks, in our shops and supermarkets, we can now make and enjoy our very own Feast from the East.

A Few
Special Ingredients

SOY SAUCE

This sauce is made from soybeans, flour and water and then fermented and distilled. There are two main types, dark soy sauce and light soy sauce. Dark soy sauce is a rich, almost black sauce which is a little thicker and has a stronger flavour, while light soy sauce is slightly saltier. I prefer to use dark soy sauce as a dipping sauce and light soy sauce for cooking.

GROUNDNUT OIL

Although expensive, it is well worthwhile to invest in a bottle of nut flavoured oil for Chinese cooking. It has a pleasant taste and can be heated to very high temperatures. It is good for stir-fry dishes, but I do not recommend it for deep-fat frying, as the prolonged cooking time spoils the taste.

SESAME OIL

This oil is made from sesame seeds and has a lovely golden colour, thick texture and a strong distinctive flavour. It is not often used for cooking as it burns too easily at low temperatures, it is more often added at the end of a recipe to add flavour.

LEMONGRASS

This is one ingredient that has just started to appear in our local shops. It resembles thick, woody grass and has a subtle lemony flavour, lighter and sweeter than fresh lemons. You can also buy it in pureed form which is easier to use.

Vegetable Spring Rolls

Spring roll parchment (pastry) can now be bought frozen, which makes the assembly of spring rolls so much easier. Don't worry if you can't find it though - just use filo pastry instead.

115g/4oz bean sprouts
1 carrot, diced
115g/4oz mushrooms, diced
2 cloves garlic, finely chopped
2 spring onions, finely chopped
1dssp oil
1 egg, lightly beaten
8 spring roll parchment skins
oil to deep fry

Serves 4

Mix the bean sprouts, carrot, mushrooms, garlic, spring onions and oil together and heat gently in a frying pan. Brush the parchment squares with beaten egg, then spoon 1dssp of the filling on top of each. Fold in the edges and roll up the spring roll. Secure the edges well, then deep fry for approximately 2 minutes, until golden brown and crispy. Serve hot.

My Chinese Soup

Everyone loves a pot of home-made soup and there's none more popular than vegetable. It is tempting to use stock cubes in soup recipes, but the results are so much better if you make your own fresh stock. Be light-handed with the chilli oil - it's hot stuff!

STOCK:
1.7l/3pt cold water
450g/1lb chicken joints
3 cloves garlic
2 inch (5cm) root ginger
8-10 black peppercorns
4 spring onions, chopped

SOUP:
115g/4oz bean thread noodles
1 carrot, cut into slices
½ stalk celery
115g/4oz mangetout peas
115g/4oz baby corn
115g/4oz bean sprouts
55g/2oz tinned water chestnuts, sliced
55g/2oz bamboo shoots
2 cloves garlic
2 spring onions (white part only)
½ inch (1cm) root ginger
1dssp oil
salt and pepper
a few drops of chilli oil
1tsp rice wine vinegar

Serves 8

First make the stock. Put the water into a pot and add the chicken joints, garlic, ginger, peppercorns and spring onions. Bring to a boil and simmer slowly for 2 hours. Try not to let the soup boil too rapidly or the chicken bones will crack and the stock will become cloudy. Skim the stock several times to remove

any froth or scum and then strain the stock through muslin. Set aside until required.

Soak the noodles in warm water for 5-10 minutes until slightly softened. Next prepare all the vegetables for the soup. Peel and slice the carrots, dice the celery and chop the mangetout and baby corn each into 3 or 4 evenly sliced pieces. Wash the bean sprouts, drain and slice the tinned water chesnuts and bamboo shoots. Blend the garlic, spring onion and ginger together in a food processor until they form a coarse paste. Heat the oil in a saucepan, add the paste and cook gently for 1 minute (do not allow to brown). Add the prepared vegetables and stir for 1 minute. Add the stock, the drained noodles, salt, pepper, chilli oil and vinegar and bring to a boil. Simmer for 10 minutes before serving. This soup can be garnished with parsley or coriander (Chinese parsley).

Prawn Toast

Toast has to be the ultimate comfort food no matter which country you live in. In America, they put peanut butter on it, in France they coat it with egg and deep fry it, and in China they opt for this simple savoury version.

225g/8oz prawns, peeled
1dssp parsley, coarsely chopped
1 spring onion, cut into pieces
1tsp sugar
2tsp corn flour
1tsp sherry vinegar
2tsp soy sauce
1tsp sesame oil
1 egg yolk
4 slices white/bran bread
30g/1oz sesame seeds
oil to fry

Serves 4

Put the prawns, parsley, spring onions, sugar, corn flour, vinegar, soy sauce and sesame oil into a food processor. Blend for 30 seconds then add the egg yolk and blend again. Spread the paste over slices of unbuttered bread, smooth the top, then dust with sesame seeds. Cut into slices or triangles and fry in hot oil for 2 minutes. Drain on kitchen paper and serve hot.

Family-style Pork Chops with Sweet and Sour Sauce

Pork chops can be one of the most difficult of all cuts to cook as the pork often dries out totally. However the marinade used in this recipe eliminates that worry altogether and ensures tasty, moist pork chops.

2dssp rice wine vinegar
2dssp soy sauce
1dssp nut flavoured oil
30g/1oz soft brown sugar
4 pork chops
1dssp oil

SWEET AND SOUR SAUCE:
1dssp oil
1 small onion, finely chopped
1dssp spring onion, chopped
1 red pepper, diced
1 small can pineapple chunks (and juice)
1dssp rice wine vinegar
1dssp corn flour blended with 4dssp water
140ml/¼pt vegetable stock
1tsp tomato puree

Serves 4

Make the marinade by mixing the vinegar, soy sauce, nut oil and sugar together. Mix well then pour over the pork chops. Leave to marinate for 1 hour before cooking. Heat the oil in the pan, add the chops and cook on a high temperature for 2 minutes on either side before reducing the temperature. Cook gently for 10 minutes, then add the sweet and sour sauce (below).

To make the sweet and sour sauce, heat the oil in a saucepan, then add the onion and cook until opaque. Add the spring onions and peppers and heat through before adding the pineapple chunks, pineapple juice, vinegar, blended corn flour, stock and tomato puree. Cook for 2 minutes until the sauce is bubbling and the colour has become clear. Pour over the chops and cook for 5 minutes. Serve hot.

Family-style Pork Chops with a Sweet and Sour Sauce

Steamed Chinese Chicken and Vegetables

This dish is very much in line with today's trend of healthy, tasty, yet quick to prepare meals. There is no nicer way to cook vegetables than by stir-frying - it retains their colour, flavour and texture. Try combining a variety of home grown vegetables with a few of the more unusual, such as Chinese leaves, baby corn and add a hint of extra flavour by the addition of lemon grass.

1 egg white, lightly whisked
1tsp cornflour
1dssp light soy sauce
1dssp rice wine vinegar
½tsp salt
680g/1½lb chicken pieces
1 clove garlic, chopped finely
1 inch (2.5cm) root ginger, chopped finely
900g/2lb assorted vegetables: broccoli, celery, mushrooms, peppers,
baby corn, mangetout, Chinese leaves and lemon grass
1dssp ground nut oil
1tsp chilli paste
1dssp light soy sauce
1tsp sesame oil
1tsp corn flour (blended with 4dssp cold water)
1tsp sesame seeds

Serves 4

Make a marinade by mixing together the egg white, cornflour, soy sauce, vinegar and salt. Cut the chicken into bite-sized pieces, then add to the marinade. Stir, then leave for 15 minutes before cooking. If you intend to use a bamboo steamer, brush the ridges with a little oil to prevent the chicken sticking to them. Place the chicken into the steamer, sprinkle with garlic and ginger and cook for approximately 10 minutes.

Wash, prepare and slice the vegetables into pieces approximately the same size. The secret in stir-frying vegetables is a short cooking time. (If you are using fresh lemon grass, either pound it down very finely or peel and squash the stalks and remove them before serving.)

Heat the ground nut oil until lightly smoking then add the vegetables. Keep the temperature high throughout the cooking. After 2 minutes add the chilli paste, soy sauce, sesame oil and blended corn flour. Cook for another 1-2 minutes. Sprinkle with sesame seeds and serve hot with the steamed chicken and boiled rice.

A Plum Dipping Sauce

This simple dipping sauce is full of flavour and especially good served with spring rolls (see page 81). It is now quite easy to buy commercial plum sauce in shops, and this greatly speeds up the preparation of this dish.

1dssp oil
1 inch (2.5cm) root ginger, chopped
2 spring onions, finely chopped
1tsp chilli sauce
4dssp plum sauce
2tsp corn flour blended with 2dssp water
140ml/¼pt vegetable stock
2tsp soy sauce

Heat the oil and lightly cook the ginger, spring onions and chilli sauce. Add the plum sauce, blended corn flour, stock and soy sauce. Heat through for 30 seconds until the cornflour is cooked, then serve.

Stir-fried Beef with Black Beans

The Chinese have a clever way in which they make rump steak a more tender cut of meat. First they place the meat in a freezer for 15 minutes. This makes the beef firmer so it is easier to slice thinly. The result is excellent, especially when cooked with a black bean sauce. I make mine from dried beans soaked overnight, but you can also use a jar of black bean sauce or tinned black beans.

2-3dssp black beans
680g/1½lb rump steak
1tbsp sherry vinegar
2tbsp soy sauce
1dssp nut oil
1dssp light oil
1dssp garlic, chopped finely
1dssp ginger, chopped finely
1tsp chilli paste (optional)
4 spring onions, sliced
225g/8oz mushrooms, sliced
2 green peppers, cut into chunks
1tsp oyster sauce
2dssp soy sauce
1dssp cornflour blended with 140ml/¼pt water

Serves 4 - 6

Cover the black beans with cold water and leave to soak overnight. After soaking chop roughly and set aside. Cut the meat into wafer-thin slices and place in a bowl. Cover with a marinade of sherry vinegar, soy sauce and nut oil for at least 15 minutes. Then cook in a wok with hot oil for 6-8 minutes or until the meat is almost cooked.

Heat the oil in a wok then add the garlic and ginger and heat for 1 minute. Add the chilli paste, spring onions, mushrooms and peppers and cook for 1 minute. Add 1dssp cold water to the chopped beans, then add to the vegetables. Add the soy sauce and oyster sauce, for extra flavouring, then return the meat and any juices to the pan. Thicken the sauce with 1dssp corn flour, blended with 140ml/¼pt cold water, and stir for 1-2 minutes until the sauce has thickened slightly, then serve with Crispy Egg Noodles (see page 93).

Egg-fried
Rice

The secret of this rice dish is the combination of oils - a ground nut oil is used to cook the rice and a sesame oil to flavour it during cooking. It is very important that the cooked rice is cold before being added to the hot oil, otherwise it tends to stick together and looks unattractive.

1dssp ground nut oil
2dssp spring onions, finely chopped
½ green pepper, diced
1 egg, lightly beaten
450g/1lb rice, cooked and cooled
225g/8oz cooked prawns or chicken (optional)
soy sauce
1tsp sesame oil

Serves 4

Heat the nut oil in a wok, then add the spring onions and peppers and cook for 30 seconds. Add the whisked egg and cook for a further 30 seconds before adding the cooked, cooled rice. Stir over a high temperature before adding the soy sauce and sesame oil. If using prawns or chicken, add them now. Serve hot.

Crispy Egg Noodles

These noodles are made from wheat flour and enriched with egg, hence the name. Although normally sold dried, you can also find fresh egg noodles in some supermarkets.

225g/8oz egg noodles
water to boil
pinch of salt
fat to deep fry

Serves 4

Cook the noodles in boiling, salted water for 4 minutes, then pat dry before frying. They will cook better if they are deep-fried in small batches. Cook for approximately 30 seconds per batch, then blot on kitchen paper before serving.

The Produce from Portugal

Y ou know it's only in very recent years that I've been able to find fresh herbs all year round. That's just one of the differences between us and the Mediteranean countries. Take Portugal for example: home of coriander, limes, lemons, sardines and much, much more. But it isn't just the produce from Portugal which is influencing our cooking, it's also the easy, relaxed Portuguese approach to food preparation and the wonderfully robust quality of their food that we can relate to.

A Few
Special Ingredients

CORIANDER

Pungent and strong, with a citrus-like flavour, coriander looks rather like flat leaf parsley, but the flavour is very different. I think it is a herb you either love or hate, but more often than not, once you get used to it, you will probably wonder how you managed without it. Widely used in Portuguese, Chinese and Indian cookery, the flavour of the fresh herb is very different to that of the seeds which are used as a spice.

CHILLIES

One of the best ways to add a little heat into your cooking is by using fresh chillies. As a general rule the smaller they are, the hotter they taste, and the green ones are usually much hotter than the red. When using fresh chillies remember to remove the seeds or, if you prefer, you can use dried, flaked or powdered chillies instead.

GARLIC

There's nothing terribly new about using garlic in cooking, but there are many new and different ways in which we can prepare it. Most people know that garlic can be chopped, sliced and diced, but how many would think to puree it or add it the form of garlic oil? One of my own favourite treatments of garlic is to roast whole cloves with root vegetables: it adds a lovely, sweet flavour to them.

Couscous-coated Crab Cakes

I feel that crab meat is very much undervalued. It is widely available, either in fresh or tinned form, and has an excellent texture. These crab cakes are coated with crunchy cous cous which gives an unusual but very tasty crust.

COATING:
115g/4oz couscous
140ml/¼pt boiling water

FILLING:
285g/10oz crab meat
115g/4oz potatoes, mashed
1dssp light mayonnaise
1 pickled gherkin, finely chopped
½ lemon rind only
2dssp lemon juice
paprika
salt and pepper
2dssp parsley, finely chopped
1 egg, beaten

Makes 8

Place the couscous in a bowl, cover with boiling water, then leave to infuse for 10 minutes. Transfer to a flat baking sheet and allow to dry out in the oven for 15 minutes at gas mark 3/160°C/325°F. Allow to cool before using to coat the crab cakes.

If using fresh crab, break the crab claws open and remove the crab meat. Be sure to remove any cartilage found in the claws. Flake the crab meat and place in a large bowl. In a separate bowl, mix the cooked mashed potato with the mayonnaise (this adds lightness and fluffiness to the potato). Add the potato mixture to the crab meat and stir in. Then add the remaining filling ingredients and mix well together. Shape into eight cakes and coat first in lightly beaten egg and then in couscous. Pat down well and put in the fridge for 15 minutes before cooking. Shallow fry each cake for 2-3 minutes on either side, then drain on kitchen paper. Serve either hot or cold with A Saucy Salsa (see page 109).

Snack-time Sardines

Sardines are so tasty served on their own, either hot or cold, but so often we fail to do justice to their unique flavour. Here are some new ways of serving this popular fish which are ideal as snacks or starters.

Grilled Sardines

450g/1lb sardines
2dssp sun dried tomato paste
2dssp olive oil
2dssp fresh basil, coarsely chopped

Serves 4

Wash and clean the sardines and pat them dry, then cook under a medium grill for 2-3 minutes, turning once. Put the tomato paste, olive oil and basil into a medium-sized mixing bowl. Stir together until a loose sauce is formed. Serve spooned over the warm sardines.

Simple Sardines

450g/1lb sardines
15g/½oz granulated sugar
30g/1oz sea salt
lemon juice

Serves 4

Wash and clean the sardines then pat them dry. Sprinkle the inside of each sardine with a pinch of sugar, sea salt and lemon juice. Pat dry again and rub sea salt on to the outside of the sardines. Place on a grill pan or barbecue and cook for 1 minute on either side. Serve either hot or cold sprinkled with lemon juice.

Sardine Paté

2 tins sardines, cooked
2dssp light mayonnaise
1dssp Greek yoghurt
1tsp chives, finely chopped
few drops Tabasco sauce
lemon juice
black pepper

Serves 4

Drain the oil from the sardines, place them in a bowl and flake coarsely. Add the mayonnaise, yoghurt, chives, Tabasco sauce, lemon juice and black pepper. Mix lightly together, then transfer to a dish and chill in the fridge for a couple of hours. Serve with lemon and hot buttered toast.

Cucumber Sauce

This tangy sauce goes well with most fish dishes, complementing the flavour of the fish with its refreshingly sharp taste.

15g/½oz butter
2 cloves garlic
½ cucumber, grated or chopped
1 spring onion, finely chopped
1tsp parsley or dill or fennel (optional)
¼tsp paprika pepper
1tsp lemon juice
140ml/¼pt creme fraiche or yoghurt

Serves 4

Melt the butter and fry the garlic until well cooked. Grate the cucumber and drain off the excess moisture. Add to the garlic along with the spring onion, fennel, paprika and lemon juice. Heat through for 1-2 minutes. Allow to cook well before mixing in the creme fraiche. Serve alongside any fish of your choice.

This sauce can also be made with yoghurt but be careful to allow it to cool completely before adding the yoghurt, otherwise it will become very thin.

Pepper-crusted Hake à la Portugal

This hake and potato dish is to the Portuguese what cod and chips are to us. I think that hake is a great fish; delicious, easy to handle and easy to cook. If you like, you can substitute the hake with any firm-fleshed white fish of your choice, but remember - the fresher the fish, the better the dish!

4 fillets of hake (approximately 115g/4oz)

SAUCE:
1dssp olive oil
2 cloves garlic, finely chopped
1 courgette, diced or sliced
1 onion, finely chopped
1 can (400g/14oz) tomatoes
dash dry white wine
1 lemon or lime, rind and juice
1tsp black peppercorn, crushed
pinch parsley
10 black olives

Serves 4

Heat the oil in a large saucepan and fry the garlic until nutty and brown in colour, then add the onions and courgettes. Cook for several minutes before adding the tomatoes, then simmer for 5 minutes.

Put the fish fillets into the saucepan with the sauce and add the wine and lemon juice. Sprinkle the lemon or lime peel, pepper and parsley on top of each fillet. Pour in the black olives and cover with a lid. Reduce the heat and leave the fish to cook for 8-10 minutes, or until the fish flakes apart easily. (The cooking time will vary slightly depending on the thickness of the fish fillets.)

Rustic
Baked Potatoes

This is a very simple way to cook potatoes and requires little attention. The potatoes are lightly steamed first, to shorten the cooking time, and then baked in the oven at a very high temperature.

900g/2lb potatoes
4oz baby onions
3 cloves garlic
few sprigs rosemary
280ml/½pt vegetable stock
2dssp olive oil
black pepper

Serves 6

Preheat oven to gas mark 8/230°C/450°F. Cut the potatoes into large dices and steam in a saucepan for 8-10 minutes until tender. Transfer potatoes to an oven-proof dish along with the baby onions, whole cloves of garlic and rosemary. Pour in the stock and sprinkle the oil on top of the vegetables to help them brown during cooking. Cook in the oven for 15-20 minutes. Serve hot.

Chargrilled Vegetables

When vegetables are chargrilled they look wonderfully golden and appetising. This unusual treatment for vegetables makes for a delicious dish and is very versatile.

2-3 potatoes
2 courgettes
2 sweetcorn
1 aubergine
8-10 baby onions
1 yellow pepper
1 red pepper
1 green pepper
1 bulb garlic cut in half
⅔dssp olive oil
black pepper

Cut the potatoes into slices ½ inch (1cm) thick, slice the courgettes lengthways, cut each sweetcorn into five pieces and slice the aubergine into rings. Lightly steam all these vegetables for 3-4 minutes to soften, then pat dry. Place them on a pre-heated grill pan sprinkled with oil along with the onions, peppers and garlic. Cook for 4-6 minutes, turning once or twice. Sprinkle occasionally with a little oil and black pepper. Serve hot on a large platter with the kebabs, and drizzle with Piri Piri sauce (see page 106).

Pork Kebabs
Piri Piri Style

Pork cooked with a Piri Piri sauce makes a tasty alternative to the traditional stuffed roast pork. It also works well with chicken and fish. This sauce can be used both as a marinade and as a pouring sauce, it is really hot and spicy though, so watch your taste buds!

680g/1½lb pork pieces
½ onion, coarsely chopped
2 red chillies
1 red pepper
2 cloves garlic, chopped in half
juice of 2 lemons
4dssp olive oil
pinch each salt and black pepper

Serves 4

Cut the pork into good sized pieces, then prepare the marinade. Put the onion, chillies, pepper, garlic, lemon juice, olive oil and seasoning in a large bowl and mix together. Put the pork into the marinade and turn it several times to ensure it is completely coated. Cover the bowl with cling film and set aside for 24 hours. The marinating process will tenderise the pork, shorten the cooking time and add a wonderfully spicy flavour. If using wooden kebab sticks, soak them in a bowl of cold water for at least 1 hour before using. This will prevent splintering when you thread the meat on. When the meat has been threaded on to the skewers, grill for 10-12 minutes, turning and basting with the Piri Piri sauce (see below) often. When cooked the pork should be tender and golden.

To make the Piri Piri sauce: heat the marinade in a saucepan for 5-6 minutes. Then pour into a blender and process. Add enough olive oil to give the sauce a pouring consistency. Excess sauce can be re-heated and served over the kebabs and Chargrilled Vegetables (see page 105).

An Old-fashioned Rice Pudding with Madeira-flavoured Apricots

A delicious rice pudding, layered with Madeira-scented apricots, which can be served either hot or cold. Dried apricots work best as they absorb the flavours of the syrup so much better. This dessert can be made with tinned apricots but remember to reduce the amount of sugar added.

30g/1oz butter
170g/6oz pudding rice
1.7l/3pt milk
rind of ½ lemon
30g/1oz caster sugar
140ml/¼pt cream
3 egg yolks
pinch of nutmeg
280ml/½pt water
225g/8oz 'no-soak' dried apricots, chopped
115g/4oz demerara sugar
1tsp orange-flavoured water
2dssp Madeira

Serves 8

Melt the butter in a large saucepan, then add the rice and stir to ensure the grains are evenly coated. Add the milk and lemon rind, then leave to simmer gently for 1 hour until the rice is well-cooked. Add the sugar, cream, egg yolks and a pinch of nutmeg to the rice. Stir well and set aside.

In a separate pan, heat together the water, apricots, sugar, orange-flavoured water and Madeira. Cook for 5 minutes until the apricots are softened. Remove the apricots with a slotted spoon and reduce the liquid to half by boiling rapidly until reduced. (This will take approximately 3-4 minutes.)

Put half the rice into a lightly greased pudding basin, then place a layer of apricots on top, then another layer of rice. Pour the reduced syrup over the top, arrange a few apricots on top and dust with demerara sugar. Place under a very hot grill for a few moments to caramelise the sugar. Serve hot or cold with fresh cream or yoghurt, garnished with a sprig of mint.

A Saucy
Salsa

It is important that the vegetables are diced evenly to give this salsa the correct texture. The combination of the vegetable juices and creme fraiche makes a lovely, tasty sauce.

1 yellow pepper
1 beef tomato
1 cucumber
1 spring onion, sliced
pinch paprika pepper
1dssp parsley, finely chopped
1dssp creme fraiche or yoghurt

Serves 4

Dice all the vegetables evenly, then mix together with the paprika pepper, parsley and creme fraiche. Garnish with parsley and serve as an accompaniment to Couscous-coated Crab Cakes (see page 97).

Caribbean Cream

W as there ever a region whose produce brought more flavour and sunshine into our cooking than the Caribbean? Just thinking of those wonderful ingredients - mangoes, papayas, coconuts, bananas, muscavado sugar, rum and spices - can make us feel more summery and banish even the worst case of winter blues!

A Few
Special Ingredients

COCONUT MILK
This is the milky liquid extracted from the grated flesh of the coconut, usually by pouring hot water over it, leaving it to infuse and then squeezing the milk out of the flesh. The clear liquid inside a coconut is not coconut milk - it is the water or juice. If you are buying a fresh coconut, it should feel heavy and you should be able to hear the liquid sloshing around inside. Coconut milk does not keep so it should be used immediately or frozen.

SALT FISH
The secret knack to this ingredient is a lengthy soaking. Ideally it should steep in cold water for 24 - 48 hours (the water should be changed several times) in order to make the fish less salty when cooked. The longer this fish is cooked, the tougher and more tasteless it becomes so, ideally it should be poached for 10 -15 minutes or, if it has been well soaked, it can be pan fried. When properly cooked, salt fish is moist, tender and very delicate.

PINEAPPLE
Pineapples when ripe can be either green or yellow. It is not necessary to pull a leaf from the top of a pineapple to check if it is ready for use - the smell of a ripe pineapple is probably the best way to judge, but do buy one that is firm, plump and has a shiny skin. When you slice a pineapple you will find that the rings from the bottom are sweeter than those at the top of the fruit.

PASSIONFRUIT
At first glance a passionfruit looks like a purple, shrivelled egg - its skin is heavily wrinkled. However, despite not being much to look at, it is one of the most fragrant of all fruits. The easiest way to use the fruit is to cut it in half and scrape out the seeds and juice. These can then be used as an ambrosial topping for puddings and ice cream or to give flavour to fruit salads.

Buccaneer's
Pepper Pot

This one-pot-dish combines a colourful assortment of vegetables cooked with spices and garlic, and thickened with tomato puree. The vegetables and quantities can be varied quite easily and the cooking time is short.

1dssp oil
2 cloves garlic, chopped
2 red chillies, chopped
1 red onion, chopped
1 red pepper, de-seeded and cut into large slices
1 green pepper, de-seeded and cut into large slices
1 yellow pepper, de-seeded and cut into large slices
1 orange pepper, de-seeded and cut into large slices
4 sweet potatoes, cut into 1cm slices
1 stalk celery, cut into matchsticks
2dssp tomato puree
pinch of paprika pepper
pinch of salt
1 bay leaf
140ml/¼pt vegetable stock

Serves 4

Heat the oil and fry the garlic, chillies and red onion for 2-3 minutes. Next add the peppers, the sweet potatoes and celery and cook for 2-3 minutes. Add the flavourings; the tomato puree, which will thicken the pepper pot, paprika pepper, salt, bay leaf and stock. Stir well, then bring to simmering point. Cover with lid and simmer gently for 15 minutes. Remove the bay leaf before serving.

Jamaican Jerk Pork

This very popular dish is full of fresh, exciting and spicy flavours. It is one of Jamaica's most famous dishes and the marinade can also be used with both fish and chicken. The longer the marinade is left to work, the more tender and flavoursome the pork.

680g/1½lb pork fillet

MARINADE:
6 allspice berries
2 red chillies
2 green chillies
1 onion, coarsely chopped
pinch of salt
2dssp light flavoured oil
juice of 1 lime or lemon
½tsp cayenne pepper

Serves 4

Remove the fat from the pork fillet and cut into strips 4-5 inches (10-12cm) long. Thread onto wooden kebab skewers which have been soaked in cold water to prevent them from burning during cooking.

Make the marinade by blending together the berries, chillies, onion, salt, oil, lime or lemon juice and pepper until it forms a paste. Use this to brush the pork strips. Pat down well, cover, and leave to marinate for up to 24 hours.

The pork can either be cooked on a barbecue, in an oven or under a hot grill. Whatever the method, be sure to turn them occasionally and baste with more of the sauce during cooking. When cooked the pork must be tender and pull apart easily. Serve with A Pineapple Salsa (see page 125).

Jamaican Bread Pudding

This exotic sounding pudding is actually very easy to make. It is the hint of spice and rum that rings the changes with this old-fashioned pudding.

115g/4oz sultanas
115g/4oz apricots
55g/2oz muscatel raisins
1 cup warm tea
2dssp dark rum
rind of ½ lemon
rind of ½ orange
2 baguettes, cut into ½ inch (1cm) slices and buttered
1 dssp demerara sugar

CUSTARD:
570ml/1pt milk
1 vanilla pod
1 stick cinnamon
½tsp mixed spice
30g/1oz soft brown sugar
5 egg yolks

Serves 6

Marinade the fruits in the tea, rum, lemon and orange rind. Leave to infuse for at least 20 minutes.

To make the custard, heat the milk in a saucepan, add the vanilla and cinnamon and leave to infuse for 10 minutes. Add the mixed spice, sugar and eggs and heat gently until the sugar has dissolved and the mixture thickens slightly.

Preheat oven to gas mark 5/190°C/375°F. Arrange the baquette slices in an ovenproof dish and spoon the fruit and juice over the top. Pour the custard over the bread and fruits, then sprinkle with demerara sugar and leave to sit for 10-15 minutes until the bread has absorbed part of the custard and is softened. Cook in the oven for 25-30 minutes. Serve with Rum and Tea Sauce (see page 117).

Rum and
Tea Sauce

This sauce can be served either warm or chilled and is delicious either way!

1cup tea
55g/2oz muscavado sugar
2dssp dark rum
280ml/½pt cream

Serves 4-6

Boil together the tea and sugar until it is reduced to 70ml/⅛pt and is slightly syrupy. Add the rum and leave to cool before adding the cream and stirring. The sauce can either be served as it is, or chilled in the fridge and then served with a rosette of whipped cream on top.

A Caribbean Curry

In this dish, I am using both the liquid and the flesh of the coconut to make a curry full of flavour and texture. Don't worry if coconuts are out of season - it is now possible to buy coconuts in cans that contain both the liquid and flesh. I like to use prawns in this recipe but the sauce also works well with other seafood or chicken.

115g/4oz shaved coconut flesh
2dssp mild curry powder
2 green chillies, chopped
2 spring onions, chopped
70ml/⅛pt coconut liquid
1dssp oil
2 cloves garlic
1 inch (2.5cm) root ginger
280ml/½pt coconut milk
225-285g/8-10oz prawns
115g/4oz fresh or tinned pineapple
1 lemon rind and juice
salt and pepper
2dssp parsley, freshly chopped

Serves 4

First extract the necessary ingredients from the coconut. Pierce the eyes of the coconut and drain off the coconut liquid. Set aside until required. Crack the coconut open and place in the oven at gas mark 4/180°C/350°F for 15 minutes. This should allow the shell and the flesh to come apart more easily. Peel off the brown skin, then shave the coconut flesh using a peeler. The recipe requires 115g/4oz so when you have enough set it to one side. To make the coconut milk, grate the rest of the coconut flesh into a bowl, pour in 280ml/½pt hot, but not boiling, water and leave to infuse. Squeeze the coconut flesh to extract all the flavour and juices then remove the flesh and set the 'milk' aside until it is needed.

Mix the coconut flesh, curry powder, chillies and spring onions together in a blender. Add the coconut liquid and mix to form a paste. Heat the oil in a large frying pan and cook the garlic and ginger for 2 minutes. Add the paste and cook for a further 2 minutes until the flavour intensifies and a little of the liquid evaporates off. Add the coconut milk and stir well before adding the cooked, shelled prawns, pineapple, lemon juice and rind. Bring up to simmering point and cook slowly for 10-12 minutes. Adjust the seasoning and garnish with parsley. Serve hot with boiled rice.

Salt Fish

You may find it hard to believe, but what starts off as a piece of dried, salted fish can end up as a wonderfully white, textured portion of fish. Salt cod and ling are the two most popular salted fish, and both cook easily and keep their shape. It is vital to soak the fish: I often leave it to steep in cold water for up to 48 hours.

450g/1lb salted fish
cold water to cover
1dssp oil
2 cloves garlic, chopped

Serves 4

Soak the fish in cold water for at least 24-48 hours to remove the saltiness and bring back the texture of the fish. Change the water several times during the process, then drain, pat dry, skin and cut into four pieces, approximately 115g/4oz in size. Heat the oil in a frying pan and gently fry the garlic before adding the fish fillets. Cook for 2-3 minutes on either side and drain on kitchen paper before serving. Alternatively this fish can be lightly poached in milk to further reduce its saltiness.

Robinson Crusoe's Banana Boats

Bananas are one of the most useful and versatile fruits: they make a quick sandwich with peanut butter; a delicious dessert when baked with a dollop of mascarpone cheese; or a light snack with granary bread and cream cheese. Children especially love them, so here is a novel way of using bananas as a quick pudding for the kids.

4 bananas
1 chocolate or coconut bar, sliced
55g/2oz small marshmallows

Makes 4

Peel back one-quarter of the banana skin along the concave side, but do not peel off completely. Using a teaspoon, scoop out about one-third of the banana flesh and insert slices of chocolate bar and marshmallows into the hole. Then cook either under a grill or in the oven.

To grill: Place banana under a grill for several minutes, with the banana skin flap out of the way. When cooked, the flap can be put back into place and the pudding can be served. The banana looks more attractive when grilled rather than baked and I find a sail made out of paper or finely chopped vegetables makes this pudding really popular with little ones.

To bake: Fold the banana skin over the packed banana. Wrap in foil, then place in a hot oven for 10-15 minutes. While this method of cooking does not look as attractive because the banana blackens, the pudding still tastes delicious!

Caramel and Coconut Sauce

This is a lovely sauce to serve either hot or cold with a platter of simple or exotic fruits. Be careful not to over-heat this sauce when cooking or the colour will become very dark.

30g/1oz butter
115g/4oz soft brown sugar
280ml/½pt water
1 cinnamon stick
140ml/¼pt coconut milk
55g/2oz grated coconut

Serves 4-6

Heat together the butter and sugar for 2 minutes, then add the water and cinnamon stick and bring to a boil. Boil for 10 minutes until slightly reduced and thickened. Cool slightly before adding the coconut milk and grated coconut. Serve warm or chilled.

Caramel and Coconut Sauce with a platter of Caribbean Fruits

Caramelised Bananas with Honeyed Mascarpone

The flavour of lightly cooked bananas topped with mascarpone cheese just has to be tasted to be believed! This is one of my favourite 10-minute puddings that looks so attractive when served in individual, tall, stemmed glasses. This pudding can be made in advance if stored in the refrigerator. The quantity of mascarpone cheese used can be halved and mixed with an equal quantity of yoghurt to give a lighter, less calorific topping.

15g/½oz butter
2dssp honey
4 firm bananas, peeled and sliced
1tsp demerara sugar (optional)
115g/4oz mascarpone cheese
30g/1oz flaked toasted almonds
sprigs of mint to decorate

Serves 4

In a small pan heat the butter and honey, then add the sliced bananas and cook for 1 minute. Beat well then transfer to serving glasses and, if liked, sprinkle with demerara sugar. Beat together the mascarpone cheese and remaining honey, then spoon over the bananas. Decorate with flaked toasted almonds and a sprig of mint.

A Pineapple Salsa

Pineapple makes a very tasty, fruity salsa. It can be made with either fresh or tinned fruit, but the flavour of fresh pineapple is wonderful in this recipe. If you want to spice it up even more, crushed coriander and cumin seeds can be added, but I prefer the flavour of this, less spicy, version which makes a nice contrast to the hot Jamaican Jerk Pork (see page 114).

1dssp light grapeseed oil
½ inch (1cm) root ginger
½ small onion
30g/1oz soft brown sugar
rind and juice of 1 lemon or lime
225g/8oz fresh pineapple, cut into chunks
few drops Tabasco sauce
140ml/¼pt vegetable stock

Heat the oil and fry the ginger and onion for 2 minutes. Add the soft brown sugar, lemon or lime juice and rind, pineapple chunks, Tabasco sauce and stock. Simmer for 15-20 minutes until the pineapple is tender and soft and the liquid has reduced by almost half. Serve hot or cold.

The Flavours
of France

I f you think French cooking is all about complicated
recipes, lengthy techniques and numerous ingredients
with strange sounding names - don't worry! That
isn't the case at all - it is simply about choosing the very best
and freshest produce, cooking it with devotion, then adding a
creative touch - a sprinkle of herbs, a pinch of spice, a clove
of garlic or a dash of wine - and that will give you the
wonderful Flavours of France.

A Few
Special Ingredients

TARRAGON

French tarragon is the more common variety of this delicate herb with a gentle, aromatic flavour. I love the flavour of fresh tarragon; it combines so well with vegetable dishes and is a vital ingredient in Béarnaise Sauce. For best flavour, use only the leaves.

CAMEMBERT CHEESE

One of the most famous French cheeses, Camembert has a distinctive flavour and can vary from mild to strong. The texture of this creamy cheese can sometimes be difficult to handle, but it works beautifully in souffles.

WALNUT OIL

A great oil to use in salad dressings, walnut oil, obviously, has a strong nutty flavour. It is now widely available and, as it is usually quite expensive, I often dilute it with a light sunflower oil as I find the flavour of walnut oil goes a long way.

GRUYERE CHEESE

One of Switzerland's most famous cow's milk cheeses, Gruyere is easily recognised by its pea-sized holes. It is an especially good cheese to cook, as its consistency when melted is very smooth and it does not go stringy.

Twice Baked Soufflé

This soufflé can either be cooked in one large soufflé dish or in individual ramekin dishes. I prefer to use the smaller dishes as this dish is very good served as a starter.

15g/½oz melted butter
30g/1oz walnuts finely chopped
280ml/½pt milk
30g/1oz butter or margarine
45g/1½oz flour
salt and pepper
¼tsp cayenne pepper
pinch mustard
2 large eggs, separated
85g/3oz Gruyere cheese
30g/1oz Camembert cheese, cut into pieces

Serves 4

Preheat oven to gas mark 5/190°C/375°F. Grease the ramekin dishes with butter and dust with finely chopped walnuts. Prepare the soufflé by beating together the milk, butter and flour, stirring well to prevent the mixture becoming lumpy. Bring to a boil, add the salt, pepper, cayenne pepper and mustard and allow to cool a little before adding the egg yolks and two-thirds of the Gruyere cheese. Mix well together, then fold in the stiffly beaten egg whites. Transfer to the ramekin dishes. Place the dishes in a *bain marie* (an ovenproof dish, half filled with water) to prevent the soufflés from overheating during cooking. Cook for approximately 20 minutes or until well risen and firm. Allow to cool in the dishes before turning out onto a greased baking sheet. Sprinkle the tops with the remainder of the Gruyere and Camembert cheeses.

At this stage, the soufflés will hold for several hours before the second cooking. Place the baking sheet either under a grill or in an oven pre-heated to gas mark 5/190°C/375°F, until they rise up again. Serve hot with a Simple Green Salad (see page 136).

Barbary
Duck Breasts

Duck breasts have now become more readily available and in this dish I have given them the simplest of treatments and served them with a tasty sauce. The flavour of barbary duck is particularly good for this recipe so do try to get them if at all possible.

2 duck breasts
½tsp salt
1dssp peppercorns, coarsely crushed
30g/1oz butter
1dssp olive oil

Serves 2

Preheat oven to gas mark 6/200°C/400°F. Peel the skin off the breast, sprinkle with the salt and peppercorns and pat down well. Heat the oil and butter in a grill pan until very hot then put in the duck breasts, skin side down. Cook for 3 minutes on each side, then transfer the pan to the oven. Cook for 5 minutes if you like your duck rare or 8-10 minutes if you prefer them well done. (The cooking time will vary depending on the size of the duck breasts.) Serve the duck breasts hot, sliced diagonally.

A French Canadian Rhubarb Sauce

This is ideal sauce to serve with duck as the tartness of the rhubarb combines well with richness of the duck. The addition of honey towards the end of cooking thickens the sauce slightly and sweetens it.

70ml/⅛pt water
2dssp demerara sugar
1 stick cinnamon
2 stalks rhubarb, chopped coarsely
1 small cooking apple, sliced
70ml/⅛pt red wine
2dssp honey

Serves 2

Put the water, sugar, cinnamon, rhubarb and apple into a small saucepan and poach gently for 4-5 minutes. Add the red wine and honey and cook for a further minute. (Do not let the rhubarb lose its shape.) Serve hot.

French-style Leeks

This is one of the tastiest ways I know to serve leeks. They retain all their colour, flavour and texture, and the cream and herb sauce adds a extra special touch. This is a wonderful accompaniment to the barbary duck breasts (see page 130).

4 leeks
280ml/½pt cream
15g/½oz butter
salt and black pepper
fresh herbs (e.g. parsley or tarragon), chopped

Serves 4

Wash and cut the leeks into good-sized pieces then place in a steamer over hot water and cook for 1-2 minutes. In a separate pan heat the cream and butter together until the butter has melted. Add the seasoning and a sprinkling of the herbs. Drain the leeks and toss them into the sauce. Heat through, garnish with herbs and serve hot.

Cassoulet

A cassoulet is to the French what a bean stew is to us and it can be made as simply as you wish. The main ingredients are sausages and haricot beans. Like many stews the flavour improves by reheating the next day.

450g/1lb haricot beans
570ml/1pt water
½ carrot
½ onion
2-3 cloves, whole
1dssp oil
680g/1½lb lamb, cut into large pieces
340g/12oz pork sausages, cut diagonally
115g/4oz garlic sausages, cut into chunks
340g/12oz bacon lardons
2 cloves garlic, chopped finely
2 onions, chopped
4 carrots, chopped
salt and pepper
1 sprig rosemary, crushed
2 bay leaves, crushed
570ml/1pt chicken stock
85g/3oz white breadcrumbs
2dssp parsley, finely chopped

Serves 6

Soak the beans overnight in cold water. Then drain them and transfer to a saucepan. Add the water, carrot, onion and cloves. Bring to the boil and simmer for 30 minutes, but do not allow them to become soft.

Heat the oil in a large frying pan and then cook each meat separately to seal in all the juices. Layer in a casserole dish in the following order: lamb, pork sausages, garlic sausages, and finally the lardons of bacon.

Preheat oven to gas mark 5/190°C/375°F. Add the garlic, onions and carrots to the same pan in which the meats were cooked, and toss around until the vegetables are coated. Add a little salt and pepper then transfer the mixture to the casserole dish and layer on top of the meats. Add the crushed rosemary and bay leaf, drain the beans and pour them on top, then add the stock. Put into the oven, uncovered, and cook for 1½ hours until the meats are tender when tested. Approximately 15 minutes before the end of cooking time, remove the cassoulet from the oven, and sprinkle with the breadcrumbs and parsley. Raise the oven temperature to gas mark 6/200°C/400°F and return the dish to the oven for 15-20 minutes until golden brown on top. Serve hot.

Simple Green Salad with a Warm Dressing of Walnut and Bacon

By gently warming a salad dressing, the flavour can be intensified greatly. This one works well when slightly heated, but be careful not to overheat it or the letuce leaves will spoil when the dressing is poured over.

1 bowl of assorted lettuce leaves

DRESSING:
½tsp mustard
1tsp caster sugar
salt and pepper
1tbsp mild white wine vinegar
4tbsp olive and walnut oil
1 clove garlic, crushed
2 rashers bacon, grilled and cut into strips

Arrange the lettuce leaves in a bowl then place all the ingredients except the grilled bacon into a saucepan. Whisk gently, then heat slightly. Add the grilled bacon pieces and pour over the salad just before serving.

Almond-scented Pear and Cinnamon Tart

This light, French-style pastry combines well with most fruits. I particularly like it with pears and served with Chantilly Cream.

PASTRY:
225g/8oz plain flour
15g/½oz caster sugar
pinch salt
115g/4oz butter, softened
1 egg yolk
1dssp cold water

ALMOND-SCENTED FILLING:
115g/4oz butter
115g/4oz caster sugar
70g/2½oz ground almonds
30g/1oz almonds, flaked
few drops of vanilla essence
1 large egg, beaten
45g/1½oz flour
5 pears, peeled, cored and quartered
1tsp cinnamon

TO SERVE:
30g/1oz icing sugar
½tsp cinnamon

Sieve the flour into a bowl and add the sugar, salt and softened butter. Cut through, then rub in until it almost becomes sticky. Add the egg yolk and, if needed, a little water to bind together to form a small ball of dough. Set aside to relax in a cool place for at least 15 minutes. Roll out to fit a 9 inch (22cm), loose-bottomed flan dish. Trim off any excess pastry, prick with a fork, then set aside to relax again before filling.

Preheat oven to gas mark 5/190°C/375°F. Cream the butter and sugar together, add the ground and flaked almonds, vanilla, egg and flour. Spread evenly over the pastry base, arrange the pears and dust with cinnamon. If the pears you are using are very firm it would be advisable to poach them lightly before using.

To do this simply cover them with water, add 30g/1oz caster sugar and heat gently for several minutes). Bake in the oven for 20-25 minutes until firm, golden and well cooked. Dust with icing sugar and cinnamon before serving with Chantilly Cream (see below).

Chantilly
Cream

This lovely sauce can be flavoured with coffee, chocolate, rum, lemon or vanilla. It must be prepared at least one hour in advance, to let the flavour develop, and all the ingredients and utensils must be very cold. You can vary the quantity of cream used from 140ml/¼pt to 280ml/½pt, depending on how much sauce you require, but you will find that this sauce whips up to double its original volume.

140ml/¼pt double cream
2tbsp milk, ice cold
2tbsp icing sugar
½tbsp vanilla essence
1tbsp water, iced
rind of ½ lemon

Place the cream and milk into a very cold bowl and whisk together until the mixture doubles in volume. This should take 3-4 minutes. Add the sugar, vanilla, iced water and lemon rind and continue to whisk for another minute. Chill for at least 1 hour before serving.

Almond-scented Pear and Cinnamon Tart and Chantilly Cream

Index

Crustless Quiche with Red Onions and Peppers

Quiche Lorraine is a traditional French dish which is now one of our own most popular savoury pies. This crustless version is one of the simplest and tastiest quiches I know, and is good with salad.

340g/12oz smoked bacon, cut into strips
2 red onions, finely chopped
1 red pepper, diced
pinch black pepper
170g/6oz self raising flour
pinch of salt
85g/3oz butter
55g/2oz bran
6 eggs
425ml/³⁄₄pt milk
170g/6oz gruyere cheese
2 tomatoes, chopped
1 tomato, sliced

Serves 8

Preheat oven to gas mark 5/190°C/375°F. Prepare the filling by cooking the bacon strips in a pan until crispy and golden. Add the onions, pepper and seasoning and cook for 1 minute. Turn off the heat and leave to cool.

Sieve the self raising flour and salt into a large bowl, cut and rub in the butter, add the bran and mix again. In a separate bowl whisk together the eggs and milk and pour into the flour. Mix lightly, then add two-thirds of the cheese, two-thirds of the bacon mixture and the chopped tomatoes. Mix well then transfer to a well-oiled, 11-12 inch (28-30cm), quiche dish. Stir in the remaining bacon mixture, arrange the sliced tomato on top and sprinkle with the remaining cheese. Bake in the oven for 25-30 minutes until firm, puffed up and golden.